CW00525936

Growing and Showing
Dahlias

Philip Damp

Best Wishes
Philip Damp
Oct / '86

David & Charles
Newton Abbot   London   North Pomfret (Vt)

Line drawings by courtesy of John Carrington

British Library Cataloguing in Publication Data

Damp, Philip
    Growing and showing dahlias.
    1. Dahlias
    I. Title
    635.9'3355   SB413.D13

    ISBN 0–7153–8600–X

© Text and photographs Philip Damp 1985

All rights reserved. No part of this
publication may be reproduced, stored in a
retrieval system, or transmitted, in any form
or by any means, electronic, mechanical,
photocopying, recording or otherwise,
without the prior permission of David &
Charles (Publishers) Limited

Photoset in Souvenir by
Northern Phototypesetting Co, Bolton
Printed in Great Britain by
Redwood Burn Limited, Trowbridge, Wilts
for David & Charles (Publishers) Limited
Brunel House Newton Abbot Devon

Published in the United States of America
by David & Charles Inc
North Pomfret Vermont 05053 USA

Contents

Introduction   5
1 The First Steps   7
2 The Early Season   13
3 Mid-season Maintenance   23
4 Preparing for a Show   32
5 The Showman in Autumn and Winter   42
6 The Showman's Calendar   50
7 Recommended Varieties   57
   Index   67

Introduction

The world of flower exhibiting is a strange enigma. The hobby of raising flowers or plants to a peak of perfection, set against self-made rules, has no other reason than a sense of achievement; a revelling in the mastery of the subject and, it must be admitted, a satisfying of the ego that rests dormant in all of us. With few exceptions, the hobby of growing and showing dahlias is confined to the English-speaking nations, such as North America, Australasia and Britain. There are no amateurs vying with each other to grow better blooms in continental Europe; whilst floriculturists in countries like France, Belgium and Holland appreciate the exhibiting skills of the professionals (and the profit motive), they still profess amazement that the amateur gardener will spend a great deal of time and money in a pursuit that offers very little as reward for such devotions!

But then, the British are world famous for their genuine love of flowers, which extends beyond the public gardens and parks with which we are amply blessed, and insists that individuals can equal or even better the work of the professionals. Thus the foundations of floral competition between amateur flower growers was set some 170 years ago, when garden culture was booming amongst the rich and influential who had the money and the labour to indulge such whims. The Victorians revelled in these flower shows and would spend small fortunes to obtain the best varieties. Having obtained them, what better way to bask in reflected glory than to compete against, even beat, your neighbour? So it was with the Dahlia, which was already a hybrid when it came to Britain almost 200 years ago. Some people believe that it is this inheritance that we enjoy today, now that ordinary citizens have gardens of their own and can follow the ambitions of their forefathers.

But there is one factor about exhibiting that the reader must understand. There is little if any material reward for a season's work, other than the sense of pride if you are successful. Prize monies are minimal when set against the annual costs of things like greenhouse heating (to say nothing of the capital outlay for the greenhouse!), fertilisers, insecticides and fungicides, pots, canes and a host of other ancillary requirements. Even at national level, a day's expenses just to attend at a show can swamp the monetary gain. So what price do you put on a silver trophy, perhaps held for just one year, or a glittering, red first-award card to frame and place on your sideboard? The answer to such a question lies with the individual, but a large part of my enjoyment comes from the friendship and camaraderie of fellow exhibitors. If, after reading my book, you would like to join them, you will find a warm welcome awaiting you.

1 The First Steps

The aspiring showman needs to understand how dahlias are classified. Firstly, they are all classified into types, that is by form; and then they are again sub-divided, this time by size. The authority for this is our own National Dahlia Society, of long experience. Its deliberations are accepted in Britain as a basis for fair exhibition rulings. Groupings by form are as follows:

Group 1 Single Dahlias Open-centred flowers.
Group 2 Anemone Dahlias Formed like anemones.
Group 3 Collerette Dahlias Open-centred, with a shorter row of petalling (the collar) in the centre.
Group 4 Water Lily Dahlias Fully-double, formed like water lilies.
Group 5 Decorative Dahlias Fully-double blooms, with mostly flat petals.
Group 6 Ball Dahlias Double blooms, ball shaped.
Group 7 Pompon Dahlias Double blooms, globular like the ball dahlias, but smaller in diameter.
Group 8 Cactus Dahlias Double blooms with narrow, pointed petalling.
Group 9 Semi-cactus Dahlias A combination of the decorative and cactus groups, ie half of each petal is broad and flat, the remainder pointed and rolled.
Group 10 Miscellaneous Any dahlia that does not fall into any of the other groups, eg those with orchid or chrysanthemum formation.

To give further assistance in classification, several of the groups mentioned above are divided again by size, ie the diameter, measured across the face of the bloom. This applies particularly to decoratives, cactus and semi-cactus (Groups 5, 8 and 9) which break down as follows:

7

1

2

3

4

5

6

7

8

8

 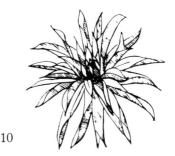

The ten dahlia forms as classified by the National Dahlia Society: 1, Single; 2, Anemone; 3, Collerette; 4, Water Lily; 5, Decorative; 6, Ball; 7, Pompon; 8, Cactus; 9, Semi-cactus; 10, Miscellaneous – example shown, Orchid (*John Carrington*)

Giant-flowered Usually over 254mm (10in)
Large-flowered 203–254mm (8–10in)
Medium-flowered 152–203mm (6–8in)
Small-flowered 102–152mm (4–6in)
Miniature-flowered Not exceeding 102mm (4in)

Size restrictions for ball and pompon dahlias (Groups 6 and 7) are as follows:

Small Ball Dahlias 102–152mm (4–6in)
Miniature Ball Dahlias 52–102mm (2–4in)
Pompon Not exceeding 52mm (2in)

These classifications form the basis of an exhibitor's planning. Classes in the show schedules correspond with these groupings, so the aspiring showman must have a knowledge of them if he or she is to avoid disqualification – which can result if a dahlia is entered in an incorrect class. At national exhibition or specialist level, most groups will be catered for, and even each size classification, so it is easy to find the correct place for your entry. However, at smaller shows the classifications are often grouped together; for example, a typical general horticultural show might include a class for 'five medium-flowered dahlias'. This would allow you to enter any of the medium types (decorative, cactus and/or semi-cactus) in that class. Similarly, a class might embrace two size classifications, stating that the exhibitor may enter 'five blooms, small and/or miniature'. This means that decorative, cactus and/or semi-cactus types can be entered, provided that they are sized as small or miniature. These permutations sometimes confuse, but if they are read in the context of the overall types and sizing, they are much easier to understand.

All of this applies only to dahlias that have been classified, which means that they have been scrutinised by the National Dahlia Society and are included in the current edition of its pocket-sized booklet, *The NDS Classified Directory* – an essential piece of literature for every showman, veteran or novice. It is published bi-annually and is not affected (as some floral lists are) by amendments; every edition is complete in its own right and cancels out previous editions. You can obtain a copy for (at present) £1.20, including postage, from the NDS General Secretary (see page 48).

The NDS Classified Directory lists hundreds of dahlias currently on the market and in popular use on the exhibition benches. However, there are still hundreds more varieties (by virtue of the reproductive abilities of this flower) that are not listed! So what happens if you are growing a dahlia that is not in the list? All of them are acceptable for exhibition, but they must be entered into the class which covers both their form and size. They will then be judged equally with classified varieties. However, in case you choose the wrong class, there is an NDS ruling which states that unclassified dahlias which do not conform to the class in which they have been entered will NOT be disqualified. Obviously, a cactus or semi-cactus dahlia entered in a decorative class, will not win a prize, but you are at least spared the ignominy of disqualification.

The Ideal Dahlia

This brings us to the requirements of the perfect dahlia, within the framework of classification which I have just outlined. In considering this, you must understand that beauty and formational perfection are not in the eyes of the beholder! The ideal dahlia is prescribed by the rules, and, whilst most of us have a liking for one particular type or colour, the showman who wants to be successful cannot afford such self-indulgence. The ideals of perfection are clearly outlined in the 'Rules for Judging', contained in that invaluable *Classified Directory*. These ideals assume that every dahlia on every showbench is perfect, until the judge arrives. This knowledgeable official then systematically subtracts faults from each bloom (in every vase) according to its form and imperfections, and the winner is the exhibit with the least faults. It would be fair to comment that there is no such thing as the perfect dahlia and never will be; and a judge will always find something within an exhibit to separate the winner from the also-rans. I have judged dahlias all over Britain and the Continent and have yet to see a dead heat!

So what are these faults – and what is the ideal? Naturally, cleanliness plays an important part; any dahlia that is marked or not fresh and clean will be penalised, and even the minor attentions of a nibbling insect will soon attract a judge's attention. Perfection of form is also of paramount importance, bearing in mind the requirements of each type: eg broad, flat petalling for the decoratives, pointed and rolled petals for the cactus types, and, for the ball types, globular petals dressed back to the stem. Formation also includes outline, that is the circular appearance of the whole bloom, which must balance with the centre to give good symmetry. The angle at which the dahlia is held on the stem is also important, not less than 45° is ideal, and, where several flowers are shown together, it is a fault to have them poised at different angles.

Colour, too, has a role to play. Good, clear hues are needed: washed-out reds or purples and fading pastel shades are to the detriment of the exhibit. Crisp colours can be the result of good culture, which is explained in Chapter 3, but they must also be well matched. Matching colours may sound odd, but the rules say quite

Symbol, one of the finest medium semi-cactus varieties, a light bronze

categorically that, where two or more dahlias appear in a vase, the colours must be similar. This sounds easy when the same variety is shown, but even then variations occur, either through cultural error or climatic conditions. Imagine the difficulties that can be encountered when a dahlia with several colours (say a bicolour with tipping or suffusions) is used. As a result, certain dahlia types which are impossible to match correctly are simply not grown by showmen. A weakness this, perhaps, in the otherwise sound rules; it often denies the public the chance to see some of the more flamboyant, even exotic, colours.

This brings me to the final point of selection. Once more the personal likings of the showman are often the last consideration; varieties that have become classical exhibition types simply must be grown if you wish to be a winner. Annual lists of prizewinning varieties lead prospective exhibitors into these channels and, as a lecturer and advisor, I am frequently asked to comment on the list of varieties that a showman holds in stock. In almost every case the list has to be altered, even replaced completely, to embrace varieties that possess all the obligatory assets.

Summing up, I have to say that dahlia exhibiting and the prospects of success are carefully regulated; but the rules are not too irksome, and they do bring some order to what would otherwise be a chaotic situation!

2 The Early Season

The successful dahlia showman prepares well beforehand. That applies not only to the soil and positioning of plants, but also to the varieties, types and quality of the eventual stock. After all, it is little use trying to win in first-class company with second-class equipment! In Chapter 7 the selection of winning varieties is explained in detail. Here, I shall discuss the importance of soil preparation, plant position and quality.

Preparing the Bed

Naturally, most of us must do our gardening on the soil that is ours by chance. There have been instances where devoted gardeners have moved house just because the soil of their garden was infertile or weed-ridden, though I feel that such occasions must be rare! The fact that you have a heavy, clay soil or a light sandy loam that acts like a sieve when it rains, does not have to dominate your thinking on gardening. Such soils can be changed, and, though dahlias will grow quite respectably in almost any type of soil, good soil husbandry goes a long way towards the creation of prize-winning blooms.

The dahlia likes to grow in a bed or area that is all its own. For some reason known only to itself, mixing young dahlia plants with other plants, eg in a herbaceous border, extracts the worst from this flower and it reacts accordingly – with inefficient growth, inferior stems and smaller blooms. A lot of it is to do with the dahlia's root system. If it is asked to compete with other, perhaps more robust, roots then it cannot stand the competition. You can make a good start by reserving a spot in your garden solely for your exhibition dahlias. As a guide, you will need 1sq yd (1sq m) for each giant or large-flowered plant and around 4sq ft (0.4sq m) for mediums and below. In your plan, separate the area where the giants will be – they can receive a little more attention than the others when you set about improving the soil.

13

Most of the preparation work should take place in the autumn after the season's crop has been cleared. That may seem but little time to bring your garden to exhibition standard, but there is a true story of a dahlia grower who uprooted an old orchard one autumn, and from the same area produced a set of twelve giant dahlias that took a national championship just ten months later! If your soil is heavy, then the autumn is the time to incorporate plenty of compost, or stable or horse manure. It should be dug into the top spit, and this turned in a forward motion so that the maximum soil surface is exposed to the winter weather. During the next few months, the action of frost and wind will bring down the soil to a friable mix, full of rotted goodness and, at best, even on a heavy loam, workable with a fork. On lighter soils, the compost or manure will help bind even the most open loams and retain valuable moisture in dry weather. You may feel that other organic fertilisers would help at this time. My advice is to leave these in the bag until the next season. Winter rains will only leach away such expensive luxuries.

By early April, the dahlia patch will be ready for its spring attentions. Choose a day when the soil is dry and the garden is firm underfoot. Wet soil compacted by heavy gardening boots may never recover, and how much easier it is for a root system to roam in an open compost than in one that has been compressed carelessly. As you open the winter-treated soil, fork back into the rows any manure or compost that has failed to disintegrate – it will soon disappear. At the same time, the whole area can receive a top-dressing of bonemeal, at the rate of 4oz per sq yd run (100g per sq m). Measure this by marking off your patch with canes, and then distribute the bonemeal evenly rather than broadcasting it haphazardly. The surface can then be lightly hoed or raked so that the bonemeal goes into the top couple of inches of soil where it will, by nature's actions, permeate into the top spit.

The area can now be left until planting time, which in most districts means the end of May or even the first weeks of June – depending on how far north you live. The reason for this apparent delay is that we are talking here, in the main, about green plants being set out, rather than tubers or portions of tubers. Unfortunately, dahlia plants are very prone to frost attack, and even a couple of degrees can set back development; severe frost can kill the plants altogether.

While you are awaiting the abatement of the season's frosts, there is plenty to do in preparation. You will find it a distinct advantage to mark out the planting positions, by setting canes or stakes at precise points, bearing in mind that the small plant you are committing to the garden in late May will, by the middle of August, have a height of 4ft (1.2m) or more and a girth of 8–10ft (2.5–3m)! Such rapid growth is the reason why this flower is popular, but you must space the plants correctly to prevent overcrowding and resultant puny growth. You will require at least 2½ft (0.75m) between the giant and large varieties, and 2ft (0.6m) between mediums or smalls. Cane positioning will mark this accurately, and you will also know just how many plants you can grow comfortably. It is advisable to turn the soil at the base of each cane regularly, to assist the immediate root movement once the young dahlia is set out, and to make planting easier.

Obtaining Stock

As previously mentioned, most exhibition plants are grown from green plants. These are obtained by rooting cuttings taken from the tubers saved from the previous season. Raised in a greenhouse, they start life with a new, vital root system, and it is this aspect which makes them preferable to whole tubers or 'divisions' of the same, that is tubers cut into pieces to produce several plants where only one grew before. There are a few exceptions to this almost rigid rule, and tubers may be used to satisfy the requirements of a particular variety. Tuber growth helps some varieties to produce very early blooms, thus meeting the need to have dahlias for a show, say, in early August or (very rare this) in late July. I would not recommend using tubers for exhibition blooms, as the multiple stems that they often produce will give the best blooms far too early for the late August and September shows, and produce second-rate (sometimes known as second-flush) flowers when your competitors are riding on first flush!

If you do not have old tubers from which new plants can be produced, or perhaps the greenhouse facility to achieve this, then you can purchase these in several different ways from most nurserymen. In April, rooted cuttings are offered for sale, and this is probably the best way to buy – they are cheaper because you have to pot up the young rooted cuttings yourself and maintain them for six weeks or so until planting time. All that is needed are a few pots,

some good potting compost and a cold frame to protect the youngsters until planting in late May or early June. A second method is to arrange for pot-grown plants to be delivered to you (or better still collect them yourself) during early May. They can then be transferred into slightly larger pots, using a good compost, and they will improve dramatically in size and leaf spread if kept for a few weeks in the cold frame. The last choice, for those without any protection equipment at all, is to ask the supplier to send the plants when all fear of frost is over. They will then arrive around the end of May or (hopefully) early June, when they can be set out in the open garden immediately. There are distinct advantages in collecting your own plants. You do not, of course, have to pay carriage charges on your order; there is no chance of damage in transit (which can and does happen, despite the best intentions); and, best of all, you can look at the plants you have paid for, and, if they are not up to standard, ask for them to be changed!

This leads us to the qualities of a first-class green plant; just what should the prospective exhibitor be looking for? Check that the plant is not diseased in any way. A listless look or pale (or even yellow) young leaves denotes some neglect during the propagation period. A tight bunching of the leaf, allied with pale-green or yellow markings on the veins, might well mean that the dahlia is virused, and such examples should be discarded at once. No self-respecting nurseryman would sell such a dahlia, as he would know that infected stock cannot grow properly nor produce the strong blooms necessary to win on the showbench. But even in the peaceful surrounds of horticulture you need to be on the lookout when buying your stock.

Planting

With a prepared dahlia patch and a stock of young potential winners, planting should be completed as soon as possible. If you have spaced, marked and tilled the plot as suggested, it is a simple task. Set the plants as close to the canes as possible, firming in the root-ball and leaving a slight depression, which is useful for

When taking a cutting from a sprouting tuber, sever it just above the point where it emerges from the tuber. Further cuttings will then be produced later on to make more exhibition plants

watering in the first few vital weeks. If a plant is 1ft (30cm) or more in height, then tie it with soft twine to the cane or stake. Later, additional canes may be added to each planting, forming a cage of three or four supports around each one. Then, the powerful growth of the developing leaf and stem can be supported easily with twine looped around the cage as it is required. After all, it would be bad management to spend so much time in the preparation of soil and plants and then find that the first gale flattened them all – along with your hopes and ambitions! Planting can be a pleasant time as the early summer sun warms the soil and young plants, and you bask in an aura of expectation, but there is also another little band of hopefuls who are equally interested in your plantings.

Insect Pests

The insect world is alive to the possibilities of that free meal you have so generously provided, and if you are not equally alive to this fact, then it will probably have a lot more than it normally gets! Insect invasions take many forms and colours, starting even before you have committed the dahlias to the open garden. In your cold frame, for example, aphids of many hues will gather to feed on the fresh new growth sprouting from the sturdy stems. Molluscs, in the form of slug and snail, are a regular menace, especially if the nights are warm after a day of rain. In June, the insidious earwig will make its appearance, and the rapacious parents are helped out in their work on the dahlias by a horde of even more destructive young.

So what to do to be saved? Greenfly and blackfly (or any other colour) are controlled, in the frame or open garden, quite efficiently by regular dousing with a good insecticide, eg one based on malathion. 'Regular' means once a week in the early season, and 'dousing' means a thorough soaking of each plant both over and under the foliage. A 'cursory swish' over the plants (as one of my old superintendents used to say) is almost useless: protection is only achieved if the spraying is efficient. Choose the cool of an evening to do this, rather than the daytime.

Slugs and snails are nocturnal predators of course, and their lack of speed on the ground is well made up for by the amount of

Set young dahlia plants close to the marker cane and firm in well

leaf, and even stem, they can devour if left to their own devices. Fortunately, we have a very good deterrent in the form of the chemical metaldehyde; most dahlia growers will know this well in the form of small impregnated bran pellets. They wipe out the attackers if heaped at 2ft (60cm) intervals around the plants. Attracted irresistibly to the bran, the slugs make their last meal on the heap, and it remains only for you to remove the messy remains each morning. Some gardens, by virtue of soil or position, have very heavy infestations, which can be dealt with by using metaldehyde in dilute form, via the watering can. By treating the dahlia patch heavily in this way, even the worst slug and snail invasions can be overcome.

Earwigs are, in truth, a dahlia-grower's enigma. Many people never see hide nor hair of them, and yet others are so badly affected by their attentions that they despair. Earwigs, despite common assumption, do not attack dahlias to the exclusion of other plants, and, if the right steps are taken, they can be controlled, if not eradicated. Take the first steps during late winter and early spring, when some of the breeding places available even in the best-kept gardens can be located and destroyed. Loose bric-a-brac left around the garden, like old timber and shrub or tree prunings, should be lifted and burned; peeling bark on trellising (a surefire hideaway) can be stripped and creosoted; and those long, tufty clumps of grass or weeds should be pulled and composted, and the ground raked clean. In this way, you reduce the places where the earwig families breed. Add to these early endeavours a further campaign against these pests, and you will find yourself in control. Repeat the regular spraying, as a matter of hygiene, but also, and here is the heart of the matter, set up traps for their total extermination! Such traps are simple and depend on the nocturnal habits of the earwig. Place small clay pots (plastic ones tend to disappear in the wind) on the top of each cane, and examine them every morning. You will find, as dahlia growers have for centuries, a collection of earwigs in each one! Disposal must be swift and conclusive: carry with you a tin or jar of neat insecticide or paraffin to drop them into.

Spray under and over the foliage at ten day intervals with a good insecticide

Watering

With the soil tilled and fertile; the plants set out neatly in spaced rows; the insects repulsed – what else remains to be done in this early-season appraisal? One most important factor is the use and application of water. It must be remembered that the dahlia plant is 95 per cent water; and any shortage of regular supplies will have a detrimental effect on growth and, in due course, quality. There are many growers who strongly believe that water is far more important than fertiliser, especially as any nutrient the plant will receive during its brief lifetime needs to pass into the system as moisture, via the roots.

When the plants are in the cold frame, they should never be allowed to dry out, as this would harden the stem and, of course, restrict development. When the dahlias are set in the open garden, their only life-support is the small root-ball which was formed in the pot. In the early weeks, this should be kept moist at all times, using the small depression created at planting time. Regular watering is essential in dry weather. The roots will then thrust outwards from that tiny root-ball, probing into the surrounding soil and building up intake to help form that powerful leaf and stem structure which will bear your dahlia blooms. Until around mid-June, use your watering can, but as those roots do start to move, you will need a hose or, better still, a sprinkler system during rain-free periods.

The early season is when the foundations of success are laid. If the preparations are made correctly, with equal emphasis on soil requirements, selection of varieties and plant form, and close attention to the first cultural needs, then the opening season will be that much easier and any quality you achieve will be a direct result of your hard work. Many exhibitors will say that the early season's tasks are those that count most, and that the summer and showtime culture are only complementary to these basics. I believe that success on the showbench is the result of a whole season's work, where each part is as important as the rest. But, as we continue the exhibition story, you must judge for yourself!

3 Mid-season Maintenance

The period immediately after planting through until the first blooms appear is usually referred to as the mid-season, although in truth it is the first eight to ten weeks of growth. In this magical two months or so, the vigour and power of the dahlia is seen to its best advantage. From a small, pencil-slim plant set out in June, the result will be astounding by the end of July or early August – a massive bush, often 5–6ft (1.5–1.8m) high and with a circumference of 10–12ft (3–3.6m). The reason for this is the efficient root system which thrusts out a wide network of feeder roots, mostly just below the soil surface, whilst at the same time probing downwards with the stronger and thicker roots that will eventually form the tuber.

The protection and enhancement of this root mass must be your main concern in June and July, starting by using the hoe well during June. In addition to keeping down the weeds, which can and do act as hosts for pests, this allows air to reach the feeder-root system. Towards the end of June, you will notice that small white roots are being cut off by your hoe. This means that the spreading root has reached the point where it is filling out dramatically, so confine your hoe to the garden shed and employ other methods to keep the roots happy!

So just how do you keep a root system happy? It needs to be protected by a mulch over the entire dahlia patch. Most importantly, this will help retain moisture (natural and added) in the plot; it will also keep down weeds and, if the right materials are used, supply nutrients to the plants. Only well-rotted manures (stable or farmyard) or home-made compost provide nutrients. A 2in (5cm) layer applied over the surface of wet soil, will soon have the roots actually growing into the mulch itself, thus gaining extra goodness and increasing the volume of root.

(*left*) Apply a mulch in late June or July to retain moisture, encourage root development and, if stable or farmyard manure is used, add essential nutrients; (*right*) Instead of manure, many growers use a covering of straw to suppress weeds and retain moisture

Stopping, Shoot Restriction and Disbudding

By the end of June, the first step in the creation of show-worthy dahlias takes place. Every plant that you have set out will have a leading growth point on the main stem. This must be removed, so that the energies of the root system you are cultivating can be directed into the small shoots lying in the leaf-axils. Within a week of removal of the growing point (referred to as 'stopping' the plant) each of these tiny growths will start to thrust upwards to form a bloom.

You have now reached the crossroads between growing dahlias for cut flowers or exhibition. If the plant is left to its own devices, it will make a fine bush and give you some excellent flowers. However, with a little more attention, you could almost reach out and touch that silver cup waiting to be won at your local show! The method is quite simple. If there are, for example, 5 pairs of leaves prominent after you have stopped the leading growth point, 10 blooms will eventually come into flower on that bush, if left to itself.

However, if the root system is asked to support less than the natural 10, you should get bigger blooms! And this, of course, is the difference between dahlias that look first-class in a vase on your sideboard, and those that look stunning on the showbench.

To effect this mid-season pruning (because that is all it is), you must reduce the shoots, and perhaps the longer stems that rise from the leaf-axils, to the point where the blooms produced are as near as possible to the size limits for their type. For example, if you are growing the giant-flowered varieties of either decorative, cactus or semi-cactus formations, then it is advisable to carry only 3 (at the most 4) blooms per plant. So if you have 10 shoots in those leaf-axils, you must remove 7 to reach your show-standard 3! It is inadvisable to do this all at once, so take them away gradually over a period of three weeks or so. Then, by the end of July, you will have a plant with three sturdy stems, each of which will give you a giant dahlia 12in (10cm) in diameter! You can grow the giants as large as possible (the bigger the better, as long as they do not get coarse), but, with the other size groups, you must be careful not to exceed the maximum exhibition limits, detailed below. For your guidance, here is a recommended pattern of shoot restriction to get your blooms to the maximum permitted size.

Large-flowered 260mm (10¼in). Restrict to 5 or 6 shoots per plant.
Medium-flowered 220mm (8¾in). Restrict to 8–10 shoots per plant.
Small-flowered 170mm (6¾in). On particularly vigorous plants, do not exceed 12 shoots.
Miniature-flowered 115mm (4½in). Do not exceed 12 shoots.
Pompon 52mm (2in). No restriction of the shoots is necessary, but they may need some disbudding later in the season.

It has to be underlined that the size limits I have detailed above are used for exhibition only (they are greater than section limits given on page 9) and, under the NDS rules, entries will be disqualified by judges if they exceed the stated limits. The one exception, as noted above, is the giant-flowered group.

Shoot restriction does not, of course, automatically give you the perfect bloom width, that is a width fractionally under the maximum permitted. In the final act of pruning, this can be adjusted up or down by disbudding. As each bloom rises from the plant, it will terminate in a bud cluster, with a fat main bud and two smaller ancillary buds below. To govern size and at the same time

obtain a stem long enough for show work, the ancillary buds must be removed at an early stage. You will also find, by trial and error, that you will have to remove more side shoots (on the flower stem itself) to lengthen it, and perhaps add that extra inch or so to the blooms.

You can see that the creation of top-sized exhibition dahlias is a combination of soil fertility, strong plants, plant limitation and, in the final act, disbudding. It is not as complicated as it sounds because you are simply adjusting the natural width of most dahlias. For example, if you know that a medium-flowered variety grows naturally to 7½in (190mm) in diameter, you only have to add an extra inch or so by shoot restriction and/or disbudding.

Feeding

To maintain the plants at full strength during this period of bloom adjustment you will probably need some form of summer feed. If the soil was fertilised well in the winter, top-dressed in the spring and maintained after planting, all that is necessary now is artificial feeding from the end of June (when the growth begins in earnest) until the immediate pre-flowering time (say mid-August).

Any of a wide range of liquid feeds or easy-to-apply granular fertilisers are efficient, but the easiest to use are fertilisers like Phostrogen or Chempak, which are both effective, fast and simple to apply. The liquid feeds are prepared by mixing the crystals (which dissolve almost instantly in water) in a watering can. This can then be fed directly to the roots or sprayed on the leaves as a foliar feed: both methods give excellent results, though the latter takes longer. A granular (larger crystals) feed is top-dressed onto the soil or mulch and then taken into the root system by the action of summer rains or your own watering. The emphasis is on a balanced feed, and most proprietary brands of artificials cover this requirement with high nitrogen (for good leaf development) and potash (for colour and roots). By mid-August when the flowers are about to appear and the buds show colour, stop feeding to avoid any undesirable softness in bloom or stem.

Disbud as soon as the first bud clusters appear, to obtain bigger blooms

Support and Hygiene

In the midst of all this activity, do not neglect the normal cultural routines. Staking or caning of the increased growth must be maintained, and, if you have adopted the three-cane, 'cage' system suggested earlier (see page 19), then your plants will be held safely within the triangle of canes and usually will need no further help. However, some of the stronger-growing varieties (especially the large- and giant-flowered types) will often, because of your pruning, develop stems as thick as a broomstick. They can easily be 5–6ft (1.5–1.8m) long, so, if they grow too big for your triangle, insert more, longer canes alongside each individual bloom. This will protect them from the high winds or gales which have a habit of springing up in late August.

In addition to support, you must practise careful hygiene routines, and give a regular spraying with a good insecticide against

Exhibition dahlias should be held firmly at all times. The three-cane system shown here allows the bloom to be tied securely between two points

aphids and thrips. Thrips, in particular, can be a menace in high summer, attacking the small buds and leading shoots and shredding them with their sap sucking habits, so that when the dahlia eventually opens, it is tattered and distorted – quite useless for the showbench.

The earwig family also have a ball in August, with a second round of personal propagation – if they are allowed access to the buds, they will do serious damage. As with the early season treatment, they can be trapped with the 'pot on a cane' routine, but there is an additional measure that most showmen adopt to protect their precious flowers. This is the so-called 'Vaseline' deterrent, where a thin covering of petroleum jelly is smeared on the top part of each flower stem, just below the bud. It sounds messy and difficult, but it is not. If a small portion of the jelly is worked into the palms of your hands, it is simple to work swiftly through the dahlia plot 'stroking' the top 10in (250mm) of each stem. The effect is immediate, as the warm summer air disperses the thin jelly covering and makes it impossible for earwigs to climb into the bud or opening bloom. This method also deters other crawling insects, like the insidious caterpillar, several species of which enjoy nothing better than a meal of your favourite variety!

Bloom Protection

By now you will be wondering if you are ever going to see a dahlia in your garden. Fear not, the product of your endeavours is at hand, and through late August and the heady month of September you will find your reward. Before that moment arrives, however, you have one final decision to make, and it is one that has beguiled showmen for years. As the dahlias open up in their full glory on your plot, do they need protection from the elements? After all, you have fed, staked and tied them and kept at bay the insect world that would thwart your efforts; but what if torrential rain or, horror of horrors, a hailstorm should appear just as the blooms are opening in perfect array? Should a protective cover or covers of some sort be erected over the plot? Let me say at once that the whole world of dahlia growing for exhibition is divided. There are those who believe that covering is essential if the flowers are to be brought to the showbench in pristine condition. Others, equally adamant in their beliefs, say that covering is unnecessary, and that better colours and stronger growth are achieved without it.

Both parties, I am sure, would agree about one thing: the giants and large-flowered types do need covering because heavy rain fills their petal cavities and will often bend the bloom head, rendering the stem useless. In addition, strong wind and combined heavy rain will mark the petals of these types and, in extreme cases, bruise them. Such marked flowers would be useless on the showbench, where clean, unmarked dahlias are a prerequisite to success. It is amongst the medium- and small-flowered types that the real controversy rages. Smaller blooms shed rain more easily and, when picked after a heavy downpour, the moisture can be shaken off easily. It is your choice, and my advice would be to experiment initially to see if the varieties you grow and, not least, your geographical position require this extra protection, or whether you can manage without it.

For those who choose to give this final piece of protection against the more violent of Mother Nature's forces, the covers can take many forms – some cheap, but others very expensive! At the top end of the dahlia cover-up is the all-over garden structure that is often a permanent feature. Posts are erected to support a sloping covering, which may be of glass or plastic. Other types have a framework which can be lifted and stored away for the winter – the covering is strong-gauge polythene stretched over the posts. All-over covers have to cover several hundred dahlias rather than a dozen or two, as the work of erection, maintenance and storage (where portable covers are used) is time-consuming as well as expensive. Remember also that, from the time that the covers are set over the growing plants, watering is entirely artificial – and with such protection going up around the middle of August, this can mean extra work in the dahlia plot for at least another five or six weeks.

The choice of covers for the smaller grower is somewhat easier. Here the emphasis is on the protection of individual plants (eg with large umbrellas) or more especially (with the giant- and large-flowered types) of individual blooms! Individual bloom protectors are cone-like structures made from strong plastic or even materials such as roofing felt. To make one, cut out a circle, 30in (760mm) in diameter, from your chosen material. Then cut out a wedge-shaped piece from the circle and fold to form the cone. The edge is pinned or sewn, and canes or wire inserted to the apex and secured, so that the end product looks somewhat like a wigwam. The whole is then large enough to cover even the largest dahlia, and can be supported above the bloom by angling several canes into the cone and then pushing them into the soil.

This form of lightweight cover is storable during the winter, easy to move from one flower to another, and very inexpensive. For one or all of these reasons it is the favourite choice of the majority of dahlia exhibitors. One word of advice: the cone must be positioned over the individual bloom as the bud is opening to show colour. As the petals unfold, make sure that the bloom does not touch the sides of the cover and cannot move about. You can ensure firmness by running a cane across the base of the cone, and securing the dahlia stem to the cane in the centre of the cone, so that if there is movement they all travel together!

So with August on hand, it is time to pick your dahlias and take them to the show of your choice – which can be as tricky as growing them!

4 Preparing for a Show

The secret of success with dahlia exhibiting (if secret it is) is that, once the blooms have been grown to the best of your ability, the final acts of cutting them from the plant, transporting them to a show and vasing them for the judge's attention must be given as much care and attention as has been lavished on them during the preceding few months. There is many a slip 'twixt garden and showbench, and it is common knowledge amongst the flower-show fraternity that lesser blooms can, and often do, beat others that should be the winners! There are several reasons for this apparent anomaly, not the least of which is sheer carelessness. For example, if you cut blooms from your garden at the wrong time, they will become soft or wilt completely; pack them hastily in inefficient containers, and they will bump against each other or lurch forward on the first occasion that you apply your brakes. You could remove them safely from your car or van at the show venue and then damage them in the hall or tent; or, as is so often the case, fall foul of the requirements of the show schedule by putting too many blooms in a vase or the wrong types in a section – both cause disqualification and a great deal of heartache! Let's look at each of these pitfalls, and how to avoid them.

When you cut blooms for a show is often dictated by the time that is available to you before the judges start their work. This period, known as the staging period, can be very short if, for example, the committee organising the event want an early opening for the public. You might have to set up your dahlias before eight o'clock in the morning, which means either a very early start or staging overnight. In either case, the time for cutting the

(*above*) An excellent small decorative, Golden Leader, showing the strong stem, balanced form and clean lines required in this section

(*below*) Giant decorative dahlias on the showbench

blooms will be affected. If you have a reasonable amount of time, then it is advisable to cut the blooms in the evening, so that they may stand overnight in deep water, thus ensuring that they take up enough moisture to last them through the show. Remember that if it is a warm day, the chances of bloom collapse are that much higher. Second best is cutting very early on the morning of the show, when the blooms are full of sap after their overnight rest, though there is still the chance that they might wilt after staging.

Selecting Blooms

The choice of blooms is of paramount importance – you will need to pick those that have no blemishes and are about at their peak. Young flowers, with underdeveloped centres and a lot of petals waiting to mature, are better left for a later date. The perfect dahlia has good depth, that is the distance from the front of the bloom in a straight line to the furthest petal at the rear. Ideally, this should be two-thirds of the width (distance across the face of a bloom), so that a small-flowered type at 6in (152mm) in diameter will need to be at least 4in (102mm) deep. Good, straight stems are essential; any 'kinks' or bends will be faulted. Colour, too, is important, especially if you are showing several blooms of the same variety in a vase – they should be as uniform as possible in colour.

Many showmen examine their dahlias twenty-four hours before cutting, marking any that show signs of being perfect on the day, eg with a small tie of bright wool, which draws attention to top-priority blooms.

At this stage, you will also need an item of show equipment that has not been referred to before, that is a set of judging or exhibitor's rings. Made in the sizes of each section, they can be bought from the National Dahlia Society who manufactures them for just this purpose. These official NDS rings are made of strong plastic and are very light to handle. When placed over a bloom, they indicate quite clearly whether a dahlia is oversized or not. If the

(*above*) A beautifully staged vase of the giant semi-cactus Daleko Jupiter at a national show

(*below*) A perfect set of five blooms of the small cactus Klankstad Kerkrade – an all-time great from Holland

bloom does exceed the limits, it obviously cannot be used as it will be disqualified and all your efforts will have been in vain.

This analysis of your probables for show can take a great deal of time until you become proficient in selection. Experienced showmen can tell at a glance which of their flowers are at peak, and even those that are oversized! Naturally, there are hiccups – sometimes a selected bloom is within the ring limit at cutting time, but after standing in water in the warmth of a hall or tent, it expands to the point where it touches those dreaded rings! Such happenings are the bane of the show world – only to be borne with patience.

Cutting

With your selection made, cutting can begin. The important thing to remember is that, from the moment that you pass your knife or secateurs through a stem, that dahlia starts to die. It is up to you to keep it fresh and vital, so your containers should have at least a 10in (25cm) depth of water, and should be standing alongside the plot so that the bloom can be placed into water immediately. To make sure that the petals do not brush against each other, fix a wide-mesh wire across the top of the container to hold each bloom firmly upright.

Most dahlias have a hollow stem, which can become blocked by an air-lock, preventing the bloom from taking up water. If this happens it soon becomes obvious, as, within an hour of cutting, the crisp petals on the growing bloom will start to go soft and eventually wilt. All is not lost though – you can still save that particular flower by making small holes in the lower part of the hollow stem, thus breaking the air-lock and allowing the life giving water to flow freely upwards. Naturally, it takes an hour or two to see if your action has been effective, but if you are cutting in the late evening and leaving the blooms overnight, then by morning you will have your answer.

Transporting

Your next task is the movement of your dahlias from garden to show, and that can take many forms. If your local town or village show is just around the corner, then you have it made! All that is required is for you to stage your exhibits (discussed on page 39) and carry the vases to the venue. With any luck, you should be able to get some help from the family.

If your event is miles away from home (top-class showmen will travel several hundred miles in search of good competition), the dahlias have to be packed securely for the journey. Preparations can be made well beforehand for this, and the various ideas that dahlia people use to safeguard their charges against the vagaries of modern travel have to be seen to be believed. Some construct racks, with rails mounted top and bottom. The bloom stem is secured to the top and bottom rails to prevent movement, and the stem stands in water, in a light plastic container (some people even use balloons filled with water).

More commonplace, however, are large tins or tubs, again with that essential depth of water. Pierce small holes at regular intervals around the rim of these containers, so that the stem can be held firmly against the side, using a pad of soft paper or cotton wool to avoid chafing. A wide string or wire mesh can also be spread over the top of each container, so that the dahlias stand upright at whatever angle they are inserted. To prevent movement at the base, put in crumpled chicken-wire or an inch or two of sand. If you are using an estate car or van, measure the height inside, and at the rear doors between floor and roof, before you pack your dahlias. Nothing could be more frustrating than to bring out a carefully packed tub of show-perfect dahlias, only to find that they are a couple of inches taller than the vehicle entrance!

Some comment should be made about the possibility of transporting the dahlias 'dry' to a show, probably laid out in boxes on soft paper, to be vased up on arrival. Some showmen do this, but it is a rather old-fashioned method and has lots of drawbacks. Firstly, it is very difficult, if not impossible, to transport dahlias in this way without bruising them, by contact with the container itself or other blooms. And then, of course, there is always the chance that they will not take water after vasing. Better, much better, to move your precious cargo in water to keep them in top condition.

Equipment

So the blooms have been selected and cut, given water and then packed for the journey. Before you depart, make sure of your

Sonny Schembri, from Kent, poses proudly with his individual championship display (for five types of dahlia) at the NDS's Harrogate show

equipment, because in addition to the flowers you need several other items. A good sharp knife; a pair of scissors for trimming; that invaluable set of rings for the final check; some packing material for the vases (eg reeds, newspaper or that excellent florists' material, 'Oasis'); vases for the exhibits if they are not to be supplied by the show society; a small paint brush to remove blemishes from the petals; and, most importantly, the show schedule and receipt for your entries if you have had to do this before the day of the show!

At the Show

On arrival at the show hall or tent, find yourself a corner where you can work quietly. Many shows provide such staging areas and tables to work on. To make sure that you get a decent spot, an early arrival at the venue is essential, as there is always a rush by last-minute exhibitors intent on beating the 'bell'. (This or the stentorian tones of the secretary will indicate that the judges are on their way!) The estimated time required, including such things as checking entries, staging and identifying varieties, is 15 minutes per vase. Thus, a six-vase entry would need approximately 1½ hours. Add 30 minutes for the unavoidable 'natter' with fellow showmen, and you can earmark 2 hours – which could be two of the most pleasurable hours of your life.

As you prepare your entries, work very closely with the show schedule, ensuring that you comply with all the requirements of the class you have entered. If the 'call' is for five blooms, any more or less will mean disqualification, and there are many disappointed showmen who will tell you just how easy it is to make this mistake. If you have chosen to grow and show decorative dahlias in the small-flowered group, you should have checked already that they are classified in the NDS list (see page 10). If they are unclassified (not listed) make sure that they conform to the type descriptions. Finally, use your set of rings again on your blooms to check that they are all the correct size, ensuring that the ring passes *cleanly* over the dahlia, the word used by the NDS in their instructions to exhibitors.

Staging

In the scheme of things, staging – that is presentation of the blooms for the judge's attention – is very low in the judging priorities. The official view is that staging must be taken into consideration by the officials and can be reflected in the final decisions taken. In effect this means that he or she will consider the other points first and then, if unable to separate the exhibits, will give the better prize to the one that is staged nicely! Judges, therefore, assess staging before they do anything else and either make a note of the order in which they have been best presented or retain a mental picture of the scene in their mind's eye! It is my belief that the latter is usually the case.

To get the best of this aspect of show work, use some of the packing materials that you have brought. Newspapers, soaked with water, or reeds, or best of all the Oasis, will hold your dahlias at good angles. If you have 5 flowers to vase up, they should all face the same direction and be equidistant from one another. The standard way to achieve this is to set 3 blooms at the back of the vase and stage the other 2 in the front, fractionally below the back row. With 3 flowers to arrange, make a triangle; with 6, the choice is two rows of 3 or (for more skilled arrangers) a pyramid, with 3 dahlias at the base, 2 just above and the last bloom at the apex. All are regular methods of exhibition and none is better than the others. After some practice, you will probably find that you are more adept at one form than another – so stick to that form as you will certainly get more skilful.

What the Judge looks for

If you are taking this sort of time over staging, what about the rest of the things that the judges will be looking for? Most of these should have been taken care of at the growing and selection stage. A dahlia for judging purposes is, strangely, considered to be perfect until judged. The officials then subtract points as they detect faults, the number of points lost depending on the seriousness of the faults. It is a very serious fault if the bloom is malformed; if it faces downwards (sometimes called 'swan-necked'); if it has been badly damaged; is limp or wilting; betrays that you have been pulling out petals (to conceal damage); has a centre which is green, overlarge or distorted (eg broad rather than round); is missing florets from the outer petalling, making it look 'gappy'; or if it departs in a serious way from its type formation (see page 7). For example, if a cactus type has petals which open in a flat way or are not revolute (rolled along the axis), it must be faulted by the judges. Each section has these definitions, listed in the *Directory*, and it is these that dominate form itself.

The lesser faults include oval, sunken or isolated centres; an oval outline to the flower; blooms that lack freshness (cut too early or not taking water); minor removal of florets; bent, weak or short-jointed stems; thick stems, out of proportion with blooms; uneven or inconsistent colouring; shallow blooms, lacking depth; blooms showing their age (maybe cut several days before the show); and the presence of aphids or other intruders.

There are several more causes of disqualification. Classified dahlias in the wrong class will get you the dreaded 'NAS' (Not According to Schedule), as will artificial support of your blooms above the level of the vase. This means that you can raise dahlias artificially by inserting short canes or wires *inside* the vase, but they must not reach above the vase. (Though how a judge can detect wires inside a hollow stem is something that remains a mystery – the thought that judges might carry small magnets to detect wires is just too improbable for words!)

It might well seem that there is a lot to go wrong, but it is all common sense really and, once absorbed by the new exhibitor, it becomes second nature – as does recognition of the good, the bad and the in-between. You have now reached the point where success or failure is out of your hands. If you have noted the pitfalls well and avoided them both in your culture and final selection then there is no reason at all why you should not be successful.

After the show, my advice is to circulate and talk with other showmen. It is the way that we all started. At one time there was an aura of mystery about success on the showbench with the classical flowers, and those who enjoyed this success would become notorious for their unwillingness to impart any information. Even a simple enquiry about culture could be met by a knowing grin and complete silence. Happily, at least with the dahlia, this does not happen nowadays. Come and talk to even the most famous of our showmen at the leading shows and they will be only too ready to offer you advice about anything connected with the hobby. There is a golden thread of friendship that runs through the exhibiting fraternity ready to be grasped by anyone who is interested.

5 The Showman in Autumn and Winter

Most flower shows that feature the dahlia in their schedule (and that is by far the greatest majority) are over by the end of September. If you have joined in the competitions during August and September, then your plot will be a little sparse on quality blooms and you will have time to assess just what the season has meant to you and, perhaps most important of all, check on the health and potential value of the stocks you have grown.

Stock Assessment

Most exhibitors 'rogue' out the plantings, retaining those that have done well during the season, and earmarking for disposal any plants that are unhealthy or have inferior colours or, as sometimes happens, just do not reach their best in their soil and situation. This latter 'roguing' is best done against a background of your contacts at the shows you have visited. It is reasonably easy to see where another grower has better stock than you have or, maybe, it has been grown in a different way. If it is a question of stock quality, then replacements should be obtained during the winter. If you suspect that the variety was grown differently by a competitor, then retain the stock but try to find out just why he or she was able to get better colour or more size on the same dahlia! You should try to make these decisions in September after the shows are over and, of course, before the plants are decimated by the first, heavy frosts of autumn.

It is a good idea to mark each plant in some way. A label with a 'star' system is a popular method: the very best of your plants are tagged as 3 star, with 2 stars for the next best, and a 1 star label for the reserves. Any you wish to dispose of can be left unmarked, and this gives you a ready-made plan when you come to lift and store the roots for the winter months.

Before lifting tubers, large stems should be cut back, preferably with heavy secateurs

Prise the tuber very carefully from the soil to avoid damage. Place the spade beneath the whole root and lift slowly upwards to free the larger roots cleanly

Core out the stem by thrusting a thin saw or drill down the centre and out at the bottom. This allows surplus moisture to escape before storage

Lifting and Storing

Lifting and storing will take up a good deal of your time in late October and November. Do not attempt to lift roots until the plants have been frosted – a mild autumn will not only allow you a longer period for assessment, but will increase the weight of the tuber growth. Naturally, the bigger and stronger the tubers, the better chance they have of survival during the winter storage period. It is sometimes argued that dahlias need not be lifted at all for storage, especially in favoured areas of the country, but showmen would refute that altogether. Possible loss apart, tubers that have been lifted, cleaned, stored and rested make a more vigorous parent root when asked to produce cuttings for new plants in the following spring. Additionally, if you leave tubers in the plot, it is difficult to dig and manure the ground in preparation for the next season.

When your plants have been frosted, move in as soon as you can and lift them in order of priority (if you have used the star system).

After cleaning, dip tubers in a solution of Benlate (fungicide) and allow to dry
before storing

45

Extract each tuber with care, removing as much of the adhering soil as possible. Do not attempt, at this stage, to clean the root completely, just probe away as much of the surplus as you can, using a short stick. Remove the tubers to your greenhouse or garden shed for a week or so, to dry out. Leave the ventilators or windows open on every possible occasion (closing only at night), and you will find that the remaining soil trapped between the 'fingers' of the tubers will dehydrate to the point where a vigorous shake will dispose of most of it.

This will leave you with a short stem, the fattened parts and a mass of small, hair-like roots. To prepare the tuber for store, trim all this surplus root away and cut back the stem to only 1in (25mm) or so in length. You will be left with a compact unit that retains all the essentials: the stem base, tuber clump and the crown (the junction between the stem and clump). The crown is the most important part of the whole root, as it is from here that most of the new growth will emerge next spring!

As a final concession to safety, the stem can be cored out. Make a small hole down through the soft, pithy centre of the stem, emerging at the base. You can do this quite easily with a strong knitting needle, a drill or an old keyhole saw (a tool I have used successfully for many years). Once the roots are trimmed and cored, they should be treated with a good fungicide to deter fungus attack – one of the winter storage problems. Benlate fungicides will help you here – I dissolve a Benlate mix in a bucket of water and then dip the entire root, allowing it to drain afterwards on the greenhouse staging. Alternatively, you can cover your tubers with sulphur dust – a tried and tested deterrent.

Tubers must be stored in a frost-free and damp-proof place. Frost is certainly an enemy if you allow it entrance to your store, but damp can be just as lethal as it causes *Botrytis cinerea* (black rot). A greenhouse or shed with a modicum of heat is usually best, but you could use a garage with a small heater. It is inadvisable to take roots indoors unless you have somewhere like a cool cellar. Roots stored in a spare room or, worst of all, in an airing cupboard, will very quickly dehydrate and die.

Pack all your prepared roots before storing them away, preferably in single layers in stout cardboard or wooden boxes. The 'legged' tomato trays are perfect for this, as the contents can be examined at regular intervals without too much disturbance. I put a layer of dry peat (dry soil, sand or ashes will do as well) in a tray and then place the roots close together (but not touching), covering them completely with more of the same material. It will be early December before you have the tubers ready for store and, as the propagating season starts again in late February, it is only a matter of eight to ten weeks that your stock will be at risk. During this vital period, look over the roots at regular intervals, say once a fortnight. If you find signs of decay (a grey mould, often on the stem), remove the affected tubers, wipe them clean with a cloth impregnated with fungicide, and then return. If the damage is bad, and a squeeze between finger and thumb indicates that the rot is in the root, cut back to clean, healthy flesh. A little bit of winter surgery should save such cases. Any such cuts that you make should be treated with Benlate or flowers of sulphur dust and allowed to dry out before going back into the box.

New Stock

With the tubers stored away for the winter and the plot turned over in preparation for next season, there is time to reflect. Perhaps you need to buy new stock, or obtain some of the new varieties that you will have seen at shows or read about in the various dahlia reviews. The best way to purchase these 'novelties' is in tuber form, but they can be expensive, so my advice, especially to the beginner, would be to 'wait and see'. Quite often, a much vaunted newcomer can perform very moderately indeed, and disappointment is that much harder to bear if you have paid £10 for a root!

Obtaining new stock of established winning varieties is not so expensive, but even with these it is advisable to shop around. Look for pot-tubers, which are almost always the cheapest and, in the view of many exhibitors, best value. Pot-tubers are sold by all specialist dahlia nurserymen, both here and on the Continent. They are small, compact roots, many not much larger than an egg because they have been grown throughout the previous season within the confines of a small pot – hence the name. You can, of course, grow these yourself – after all, they are only a plant which has not been set out in the open garden. Their size and reduced weight make them very useful to the trade because the cost of packaging and postal charges is reduced. The smallness of the pot roots does not diminish their vitality, in fact the reverse is usually the case, with the tiny pot roots coming into growth quicker than the big tubers when propagating starts in February. If you want to see just what a pot-tuber looks like, you will find examples in any garden centre, superstore or nursery from January onwards. They are contained in polythene packs so that you can easily see the contents. Most of these are from Dutch or Dutch-owned nurseries – in 1983 some 50 million of these tiny harbingers of beauty were exported by our horticultural friends in the Netherlands.

Your next question could well be, 'Are the pot-tubers sold in garden centres and the bigger stores good for exhibition?'. The answer has to be no, but not because the quality is suspect – it is not. The mass-produced varieties for the general market, with a few exceptions, are better as garden or cutflower types than for the showbench. When you consult my list of recommended varieties, or accrue a list of your own, you will certainly find that very few are generally available. Most will be exclusive to a specialist catalogue, although many nurserymen who list other floral subjects, eg chrysanthemums and fuchsias, will have a comprehensive listing of exhibition dahlias. So, it is best to buy from a specialist dahlia supplier, or a nurseryman with some knowledge of show types.

Camano Choice, a small, lilac-pink decorative from the USA

Naturally, the best stock will not be cheap, but then a good healthy variety which retains its health for a long period is a much better investment. As you become more involved in exhibiting, your own stock could well be in demand. Other exhibitors may want tubers of your varieties and will be ready and willing to exchange. Such machinations have oiled the wheels of the dahlia world for a century or more!

Other Information

Soil and stock assessments apart, the winter period is also a time for increasing your general knowledge of exhibiting. Study schedules of shows in which you have an interest, and join the National Dahlia Society and (where available) your local society. The literature offered by the NDS to members is crammed full of interest for the exhibitor, with special analyses and trials' results in the *January Bulletin*. The General Secretary's address is 26 Burns Road, Lillington, Leamington Spa, Warwickshire CV32 7ER, and the subscription (1985) is £5.98 (inc VAT). You will also be able to obtain such necessary items as the previously mentioned *Classified Directory* (which includes recommended varieties for exhibition), sets of exhibitor's rings, a cultural guide and the famous summer production *The Dahlia Annual*. Some of these items are free of charge to members, with a small charge for non-members.

You will need to consider the purchase of strong canes, a reliable sprayer, trays, pots, soil and a large soundly built cold frame (essential for the exhibitor). Winter, or the 'close' season, is an invaluable opportunity to make all your preparations – the successful exhibitor is always well equipped and prepared in advance.

6 The Showman's Calendar

November

The showman's year starts this month when plants are frosted, lifted, cleaned and stored preparatory to the new season ahead.

Remember to discard the varieties which have not served you well, and make a note to obtain fresh supplies of any stock that disappointed. When conditions allow, clear the dahlia plot of the season's residue, and rough dig thoroughly. Clean and store your canes or stakes, and pack away any covers that are portable.

December

Examine your tubers in store. If any show signs of rot, cut away the infection, treat with a fungicide and return to store.

The dahlia reviews and results of shows and trials are available this month. Study them well to keep abreast of the latest newcomers and the varieties that have done well, particularly in your own area. If weather conditions allow, dig over the dahlia plot to leave maximum surface exposure for the benefit of winter frosts. Any compost that you have made in the summer and autumn should be well rotted by now, and this should be trenched into the plot as you progress. If you are fortunate enough to lay your hands on a supply of mature stable or farmyard manure, mix this in with your own home-made compost!

Remind your family that you would like the latest dahlia book, tuber of a new variety, a bag of potting compost or anything else that will fit into your stocking!

(*above*) Medium decoratives range up to 8in (203mm) in width and make perfect exhibition material. This yellow seedling has been staged in the popular 2 on 1 pattern

(*below*) Miniature ball Rothesay Superb, ready to be cut for show

January

As the New Year dawns, priority should be given to the tubers in store, and a thorough examination is vital every few weeks from now on until you eventually commit them for propagation.

Clean and prepare the greenhouse, washing pots, trays, staging, tools and glass with disinfectant. Diluted Jeyes Fluid is ideal for this job. Check on your supplies of peat, compost, potting sand, and give special attention to your heating. If you are using electricity or gas heaters operating on a thermostat, carry out a few tests to ensure that they are working correctly.

Purchase new tuber stock now.

February

This month sees the start of the dahlia showman's propagating year. Set up the overwintered tubers alongside the new purchases. Watch carefully for predators; even in the best conducted greenhouses, aphids will appear and slug eggs, often concealed in the old roots, will hatch and become a nuisance. Bait the boxes or trays with slug pellets to ensure that the new growth (appearing around the end of the month) will grow healthily and undamaged. Check on non-sprouting tubers, and replace quickly with new stock.

March

Cuttings can be taken this month when the new growth is around 2–3in (5–7cm) long. If the weather is sunny, shade the cuttings in the propagator or on the open staging.

Towards the end of the month, the first batch of rooted cuttings will be ready to pot on. Remember that the rooting mixture of peat and sand contains no nutrient – so give the new plants a good compost in which they can grow strongly.

(*above*) Large cactus and semi-cactus in a two-vase class. Note the chevron staging of the central exhibit, each vase being 2 on 1

(*below*) The giant semi-cactus Super, ready to be cut for the show. Note the balance between the centre and the outline, which can bring success in close competition

April

Continue taking cuttings, and move into larger pots or boxes those that have outgrown their first potting.

If you have taken enough cuttings of your chosen varieties, divide the stock roots into pieces, potting them into deep boxes or trays to be used later on as replacements or stock.

Towards the end of the month, move plants into the cold frame where they can harden off for a few weeks preparatory to planting out at the end of next month.

Turn your attention to the dahlia plot. Fork over the entire area, breaking up the soil into a friable condition, and trenching back any compost that has not broken down completely into the soil. Apply bonemeal over the whole plot at the rate of 4oz per sq yd (100g per sq m)

May

Unsprouted tubers can be set out in their flowering positions from the first week. Spray the plants in the cold frame to keep pests at bay and watch out for slugs, baiting them if they become a nuisance.

Mark out the dahlia plot with 'marker' canes, and work the soil at the base of each one to assist early root movement when the plants are eventually set out.

Start planting towards the end of the month when all fear of frost is over. Watch for sproutings from tubers set out earlier in the month, and protect these, if necessary, from any snap frosts. Bait with slug pellets as soon as the dahlias are in position, and start a regular programme of spraying to keep away other predators.

June

A busy month, with lots to do. Developing plants need to be secured to their supports, with extra canes added if necessary. Growing points should be removed from all plants by the end of the month to encourage side shoot growth and bushiness.

Keep down weeds by regularly hoeing the plot; watch carefully for the feeder roots, and stop hoeing as soon as the first signs are noticed.

Watch for earwigs; June is the peak month for their attentions.

Morley Lass, a small, pale-yellow semi-cactus – and a future winner

Dispose of them by trapping, and continue with the regular spraying against aphids. Water regularly when nature doesn't oblige. Obtain, stack and prepare materials for the all-important mulching.

July

Mulching can take place from early this month, covering, if possible, the entire area where your show dahlias are being grown. Continue tying-in the fast-developing plants and begin restricting side shoots (laterals) to bring each plant into line with the type of dahlia that you are growing. Towards the end of the month, start disbudding, eventually reducing the 'bud-cluster' to the central bud.

Continue plant hygiene and see that all the plants are amply supplied with water. Liquid feeding, either by foliar spraying or via the watering can, should start from the beginning of the month. Continue until late August, with the emphasis on high nitrogen feed, until changing to one with high potash at that time.

Check the show dates, venues etc, for the events that you intend to visit. Write for the show schedules if they have not been received.

August

Showtime is on hand! Erect covers to protect the blooms and continue disbudding, taking care that you keep within the section size limits.

Prepare your vases, bloom tubs, rings etc, ready for your first expedition to the show.

Do not forget in all the excitement of achievement to continue with plant spraying against insect attack. Similarly, remember the regular feeding of the plants. Practise vasing and staging your dahlias at home to make you more proficient when you get to the show. Dust off the sideboard ready to receive the silver trophies and framed prize cards!

September

Continue with the routines of spraying, feeding and watering even though you are busy at the shows.

Later in the month, make a stock evaluation, marking those plants which have done well in your garden, noting those that have failed for any reason, eg disease, colour loss or inefficient growth. Talk to other showmen, and make a note of any information which will benefit you next year.

October

The shows are over, and fairly soon the plants will be frosted. Prepare for the lift-and-store operation, ensuring that you have enough boxes for packaging, and peat or other materials to cover the roots during the winter, and that your storage area is clean, dry and ready to receive the precious stocks.

7 Recommended Varieties

Dahlias that are generally successful at British shows have a decided tendency to become regionalised, that is to be better in one area of the country than another – where climatic conditions vary, so does the performance of a flower. The biggest differences are shown in the types that are successful in the South and the North, with 'favourite' winners in, say, the London area being often quite hopeless in Scotland or the North of England. Analyses of show winners help considerably, especially those produced by the local societies, eg the Scottish Chrysanthemum & Dahlia Society which reflects almost 100 per cent the local trend in Scotland. National show analyses compiled by the NDS from its shows held in London and Yorkshire would seem to offer a solution, but in truth they do not, because nowadays, with exhibitors bringing their blooms long distances, winning varieties in London can well have been grown in Devon or Northumberland; and the Harrogate (Yorkshire) analysis will often contain varieties that have been grown in Surrey or Kent. Happily, there are many exceptions to this general rule, and these 'classicals' have proved themselves over many years to be equally at home anywhere in the country. It is some of these that I offer here, with my comments on their abilities.

Alva's Supreme A pale-yellow giant decorative from New Zealand that grows and wins well anywhere. Reasonably easy for the beginner.

Nina Chester Small decorative, white with exquisite form. An absolute must for the showman in this group.

Cryfield Bryn Raised in the Midlands, this small semi-cactus in bright yellow does have some health problems, but has perfect form.

Lady Linda Fairly recent, a small yellow decorative, on powerful stems and with very formal petal 'lay'.

Sherwood Standard An orange medium decorative from Nottinghamshire, recently arrived on the scene, but already well established.

Eastwood Moonlight One of the best of the many medium semi-cactus. A yellow raised in Essex with a string of successes.

Kidd's Climax A veteran giant decorative in cream, pink and yellow shades. Easy to grow, comes from New Zealand.

Reginald Keene The parent of several colour sports, this large semi-cactus, with orange and flame blends, has classical form and wins nationwide. British raised, the sports in salmon and pink are just as good as Dad!

Hallmark An elegant pompon, blended lilac and dark pink. One of the best of the modern show poms.

Moorplace A rich, royal-purple pompon that grows to show perfection with ease. Early blooms sometimes oversize, so some care needed.

Athalie From Derbyshire, this dark-pink pure cactus is a regular winner. Another for the beginner, it is healthy and virtually grows itself.

Silver City A very old dahlia in terms of showbench choice. A large decorative, clear white on strong stems. Another from the Midlands.

Risca Miner A ball dahlia, small group, purple-red. A recent arrival with such form that it was taken to showmen's hearts and collections immediately!

Symbol One of the true classical dahlias, which has been winning medals and cups for 25 years or more. An orange medium semi-cactus from Holland. Again, one with several colour sports that vie for attention with the parent: salmon, pink, rose etc, all known by the original name with a descriptive prefix.

Bonaventure From the veteran to the new boy – this massive giant decorative (orange blends) has just arrived from the USA and has startled showmen with its winning form. Still expensive, but worth the cash.

Suffolk Bride A white medium semi-cactus from East Anglia. A regular workhorse, which rarely lets you down.

Almand's Climax From Almands' Dahlias, California, this pink-blend sport of the New Zealand Kidd's Climax (see above) is first class. A giant of large proportions, it grows readily anywhere in the country.

Mark Willo Shades of pink for this pompon with the winning ways. A nice easy one to start with and a fine record to back it up.

Ruskin Avenger A top seedling winner on its recent introductory season, it has now established an international record. Medium semi-cactus, yellow, with classical form. Good in the North, where it was raised.

Evelyn Foster This white medium decorative from the USA has been around for some time, but it still manages to win. A tall grower, it does have some trouble with petal form, but when grown correctly is hard to beat.

Hamari Girl A pink giant decorative that should be on every showman's list. Raised by Surrey's international expert, 'Pi' Ensum, the Hamari strains have won every award possible in the dahlia world.

Frank Hornsey Not as formal as some of the other small decoratives, but this orange beauty and any of its several colour sports (yellow, rose, cream and pink to mention but a few) have a group of devotees who would never desert them!

Kiwi Brother British-raised, despite the name. A delicately shaped small semi-cactus in an odd blend of pink and bronze. Does well in the south.

Willo's Violet 'Willo' is the prefix of the world's leading pompon raiser, the late Norman Williams from Australia. Any 'Willo' pom is a good pom, and this one, colour as name, is no exception.

Orange Hornsey, the sport (mutation) of the famous bronze exhibition dahlia, Frank Hornsey

Wootton Cupid The 'Wootton' varieties are from Warwickshire's Les Jones, with many such prefixed varieties to his name. This one is a small ball variety in rosy pink.

Klankstad Kerkrade Perhaps the finest of all the exhibition dahlias, and with a 25 year record of domination in the small cactus group. You must have this yellow; it is an easy-to-grow winner.

Majestic Kerkrade A sport from famous KK (above), this one hails from the USA and is predominantly pink. Just as good as the parent, and possibly a little healthier in stock terms.

Abridge Taffy A beautifully formed white miniature decorative that took a major trials award for raiser Jack Kinns (Essex) in Germany in 1983. Now, of course, internationally famous.

Hamari Gold The very latest from top raiser Ensum – a giant decorative in deep golden-bronze with immaculate form. A sensation at the 1984 National Dahlia Show in London; on release in 1985.

Banker A medium cactus from Holland. Colour is flame-red on excellent stems. Not many in this section, but this is probably the best.

Mark Damp This apricot-and-pink blended large semi-cactus is named after the author's grandson. It has excellent show form and powerful growth and stems. First rate for exhibition at any level.

La Cierva Of collerette form – the back petals are purple with white tips, the inner white. An acknowledged and proven winner in this rare group.

Comet This dark-red anemone variety and its lighter sport, *Scarlet Comet*, are the best in the group. A rare section, but these could be used, for example, in a class for 'Any Other Variety', often seen at smaller shows.

Daleko Jupiter A really big giant semi-cactus and very easy to grow. Colour is a combination of red and yellow and there is now a pink sport, *Pink Jupiter*, that gives you a matching pair for show.

Downham Royal A purple miniature ball that has excellent show form, and stems to match. A favourite with many exhibitors.

Inca Dambuster 'Inca' is the prefix of Birmingham raiser George Brookes, who has a lifetime of successes behind him. Dambuster, a massive lemon-yellow giant semi-cactus, is perhaps one of his best.

Polyand A lilac-pink large decorative with formal petalling. Strong stems make this Australian variety one of the best in the group.

Rokesley Mini This falls into the miniature cactus group, which is very short of good contenders. White is perhaps the best in the group.

Shy Princess A tall growing, white medium cactus – a real beauty, and a recent arrival from Hertfordshire.

The Master A real workhorse giant decorative bronze, grown by most fanciers of the 'big boys'; wins prizes everywhere.

White Klankstad A sport of famous *Klankstad Kerkrade* (yellow). This one, in the view of many growers, is better now than its parent. Form is pure cactus, and it hails from Scotland.

Clair de Lune Dutch and a form-perfect collerette for show. Shades of yellow throughout as the name might suggest.

William John A red-and-orange pom of excellent form. Plenty of bloom for this Australian introduction that is grown by many of the top pom exhibitors.

The foregoing gives a taste of the varieties available for show work. There are many regional alternatives that can be as good as (and sometimes better than) those that enjoy a national reputation for reliability.

When making your choice, you should always try to keep abreast of the latest developments. For members, the National Dahlia Society not only prints those helpful analyses, but offers an advice service to locate stocks of varieties.

My Suggested Six Varieties for the Beginner

For the new showman, aiming to win a prize or two at the local show, here are six dahlias that should give first-class results when grown for the first time.

Lady Linda Small decorative, yellow.

Nina Chester Small decorative, white with occasional lavender flush.

Alva's Supreme the best giant for the beginner. Yellow, with easy to grow habit needing no special attentions.

Klankstad Kerkrade A prolific winner, which attains winning form under the most difficult of soil and weather conditions. Pale yellow in the small cactus group.

Symbol An orange medium semi-cactus that will grow anywhere. Reaches maximum size with ease. A delight to grow.

Willo's Violet An Australian pompon that finishes in the required globular form almost without assistance! Colour as name and a delightful growth habit.

Future Winners

Every season the dahlia produces a host of new seedlings that emanate from the small army of hybridists, both amateur and professional. Amongst hundreds that reach our notice, there are some that can and do make the grade as exhibition varieties of substance. There are a great many more that are only passable, but the greatest number of all are the newcomers which their raisers believe are swans when, in truth, they are just geese! The dissemination of such novelties is the subject of annual reports and analyses by dahlia journalists nationwide; it is an interest which has been amongst my seasonal responsibilities for thirty years or more, and I would be the first to say that a great deal of the success of such forecasts depends on soil, situation and method of cultivation, in addition to the obvious experience that such journalists bring to their task. To advise readers that a new dahlia is a world beater is a rare occurrence, although it does happen occasionally! Most recommendations would be tagged as 'promising' or 'possessing potential' based on comparisons with similar varieties that have already proven their worth. In approaching this list of 'future winners', such considerations have been uppermost in my mind!

Morley Lass A major seedling winner at the National Dahlia Society's London Show. A pale yellow, small cactus variety with the form to win prizes anywhere. I liked its firm, strong habit, and the raiser, Neville Weekes from Leeds, tells me that it is very healthy and a good tuber maker – two front-line assets.

Hamari Accord This rates consideration as a potential winner in the eighties. Yet another national seedling winner, this time with the country's top award in 1983 – the Jescot Trophy at London. It is a well-formed medium semi-cactus in pale lemon. It is a pity that most of our top winners appear to come in that particular colour, but in considering such future winners, colour, provided it is good, is less important than form.

Recommended Varieties

Kenilworth A brand-new medium decorative in bright red comes into a section that could well benefit from an influx of quality varieties. This one is not easy to grow to perfection, as the bloom angles are difficult to control. Master this, however, and it is a dahlia with a future.

Cryfield Rosie One of the best ball dahlias to appear for a number of years. It is a delightful colour blend, being mid-yellow overlaid lavender, and the petals curve back to the stem in the required form. I was particularly impressed when growing this lovely newcomer on trial last summer.

Page Boy Also in the ball group, although unclassified (like the others in my 'futures' list), this will be sized as a miniature in all probability. Colour is a deep purple on elegant stems. There is plenty of competition in this section, but *Page Boy* will hold its own I am sure.

White Linda Most showmen would accept that Lady Linda (yellow) is a top variety in the small decorative group, and it follows that this

The pale-yellow Hamari Accord illustrates beautifully the form of a semi-cactus

The purple decorative Betty Bowen. Note the depth and immaculate form of these blooms

white sport should be as good. It swept in with a blaze of publicity in 1983, and in my opinion has lived up to every promise. It goes top of my list for future recommendation.

Spencer Named after the Princess of Wales' family, this is another excellent small decorative, in light mauve pink. Strong stems, perfect symmetry, and a prolific habit puts it on my list of future winners. Grown by Northampton's Norman Lewis, one of our leading hybridists.

Bonny Brenda A new miniature decorative, bright orange-red. In my trials it bloomed consistently from late July until October. Almost every bloom could have been cut for show work, and there can be no better recommendation for a dahlia with a future!

'Pi' Ensum with his lovely new giant decorative, Hamari Gold

Betty Bowen This purple (lighter reverse) is included because I feel it has everything that a modern dahlia requires. It will grow to a winning form with ease on a powerful bush that offers scores of blooms throughout the season. In other words, it is a dual purpose variety, good for everyone!

Index

Air lock, 36
Ancillary buds, 25, 27
Anemone dahlias, 7
Angles (stem), 39
Aphids, 19, 29, 40, 55
Artificial fertiliser, 27; support, 40
Ashes, 47

Ball dahlias, 7, 11
Balloons, 37
Benlate, 44, 46, 47
Blackfly, 19
Bloom protection, 29–31
Bonemeal, 14, 54
botrytis cinerea, 46
Bud cluster, 55

Cactus dahlias, 7, 9, 10, 11, 25, 40
Cage system, 28
Cane positioning, 15, 19
Caning, 28, 49
Caterpillars, 29
Centres, faults of, 40
Chempak, 27
Classified Directory, 10, 48–9
Cold frame, 17, 19, 22, 49, 54
Collerette dahlias, 7
Colour, 11–12, 35, 40, 42, 56
Compost, 14, 23, 50, 53
Containers, 32, 36, 37
Coring, 44, 46
Covers, 29, 30–1, 55
Crown, 46
Cultural Guide, 49
Cuttings, 17, 35, 36, 53, 54

Dahlia Annual, The, 49
Decorative dahlias, 7, 9, 10, 25, 32, 39, 65
Depth of bloom, 65
Disbudding, 24, 27, 55
Disease, 17, 46, 47
Disqualification, 32, 36, 39

Early blooms, 15
Earwigs, 19, 20, 29, 54
Entries, show, 39
Equipment, show, 37
Exhibitor's rings, 35, 49

Faults, show, 40–1
Feeder roots, 23
Feeding, 27, 55
Fertilisers, 27
Flower of sulphur, 47
Foliar feeding, 27
Form, 11
Frost attack, 14
Fungicide, 46, 47, 50

Garden centres, 48
Giant-flowered dahlias, 9, 13, 15, 25, 28, 30
Granular feed, 27
Greenfly, 19
Greenhouse, 46
Green plants, 14, 15, 17

Harrogate Show, 38
Hoeing, 23, 54
Hollow stems, 36, 41
Hose, 22
Hybridists, 63

Insecticides, 19, 20, 28
Insects, 19

January Bulletin, 48
Jeyes Fluid, 53
Judging, 35, 39, 40–1

Large-flowered dahlias, 9, 25, 28, 30, 53
Lifting & storing, 42, 43, 44–7, 56
Liquid feeding, 27, 55

Malathion, 19
Manures, 14, 23, 24, 44, 50

Medium-flowered dahlias, 9, 15, 25, 30, 35
Metaldehyde, 20
Miniature ball dahlias, 9
Miniature-flowered dahlias, 9, 25
Miscellaneous dahlias, 7
Mould, 47
Mulching, 23, 24, 27, 55

NAS (Not according to schedule), 40
National Dahlia Society, 10, 25, 35, 39, 48, 57
Newspaper, 38, 39
New stock, 47
Nitrogen, 27, 55
Nurserymen, 47, 48

Oasis, 38, 39

Packing, 37, 38
Paraffin, 20
Peat, 47, 53, 56
Petroleum jelly, 29
Phostrogen, 27
Planting, 15, 17–19
Plastic containers, for transporting, 37
Pompon dahlias, 7, 9, 25
Portable covers, 30
Potash, 27, 55
Pot-grown plants, 17
Potting composts, 17
Pot tubers, 47, 48
Prize cards, 55
Propagating, 53
Protection, bloom, 29–31
Pruning, 25, 28
Pyramid staging, 40

Racks, for transporting blooms, 37
Reeds, 38, 39
Reviews, 47
Rings, exhibitors, 35, 36, 38, 39, 55
Rogueing, 42
Rooted cuttings, 15, 53
Root systems, 23, 25, 27

Sand, 47
Scissors, 38
Scottish C & D Society, 57
Semi-cactus dahlias, 7, 9, 10, 25, 64
Shoot restriction, 24, 25–7
Show hall, 38
Showman's Calendar, 50
Show schedule, 32, 38, 39, 42, 48, 55
Side shoots, 55
Silver trophies, 55
Single dahlias, 7
Size, 7–8, 25–7, 35–6, 42
Slugs and snails, 19, 53, 54
Small-flowered dahlias, 9, 15, 25, 30, 35, 39
Soil preparation, 13–15, 27
Specialist catalogues, 48
Spraying, 20, 28–9, 49, 55
Sprinklers, 22
Staging, 32, 36, 38, 39–40, 55
Staking, 28
Star system, 42, 44
Stems, 40
Stock evaluation, 56
Stopping, 24–5
Swan-necks, 40
Symmetry, 11

Thrips, 29
Tomato trays, 46, 49
Top dressing, 14, 27
Transporting blooms, 32, 36–7
Trenching, 54
Trials, 50
Tubers, 14, 15, 17, 23, 43, 44, 46ff, 53, 54
Tubs, 37

Unclassified varieties, 39

Vasing for show, 37, 41, 55
Vaseline, 29

Watering, 22, 55
Water lily dahlias, 7
Winter storage, 44, 46–7
Wire, 36, 37